Lights, Camera, Transcription! — How to Build a Video-to-Text Machine That's Smarter Than Your Study Notes

CHAPTER 1 : From Lost & Confused to Cloud-Deployed: A Developer's Comedy on Turning Videos into Smart Transcripts (With Extra Drama from Java, Python, and Git)

Revisiting course material after watching tutorial videos can sometimes feel like a comedic endeavor.

1. The Overconfident Learner: After watching the tutorial, you feel like a genius. But when you sit down to revise, it's like:

"Wait, was that in the video? Or did I dream about it?"

2. The Note-Taking Dilemma: You took notes during the video, but now they look like:

"Hieroglyphics deciphered by a caffeinated squirrel."

3. The Distraction Magnet: Every time you try to revise, suddenly everything else becomes interesting:

"I should clean my room... and maybe reorganize my sock drawer."

4. The Memory Blackout: You remember the instructor making a crucial point, but:

"It's like trying to recall a dream after waking up—blurry and elusive."

5. The Infinite Loop: You rewatch the video to understand a concept, but end up:

"Caught in an endless cycle of pausing, rewinding, and questioning your life choices."

When AI Becomes Your Study Buddy

The Struggle is Real

Ever tried revisiting a tutorial video, only to realize your memory has filed it under "Lost & Found"? It's like your brain decided to play hide and seek with the information.

Enter AI: Your New Best Friend

Imagine having an AI-powered assistant that not only transcribes your videos but also adds timestamps. It's like having a personal secretary who never sleeps, doesn't require coffee breaks, and doesn't judge your binge-watching habits.

Keyword Search: Because Scrolling is So 2020

With timestamps, searching for that elusive "how-to" moment becomes a breeze. Just type in a keyword, and voilà! You're transported to the exact moment in the video. It's like having a teleportation device for your learning needs.

Deploying to the Cloud: Because Your Laptop Deserves a Break

Why burden your personal computer when you can harness the power of the cloud? Deploying this solution to platforms like Google Cloud Platform (GCP) ensures scalability, reliability, and most importantly, gives your laptop a much-needed rest.

The Grand Finale

So, next time you're drowning in a sea of tutorial videos, remember: with AI transcription and cloud deployment, you're not just surviving—you're thriving. And who knows? Maybe one day, your AI assistant will even laugh at your jokes.

Lights, Camera, Code! Building a Video-to-Transcript Saga

Ever wished your videos could just spill the beans in text? Let's embark on a whimsical journey to craft a magical machine that turns videos into searchable transcripts with timestamps. And yes, we'll launch it into the cloud—because why not?

Step 1: The Grand Blueprint

Imagine a contraption that:

- **Listens** to your videos like an attentive student.

- **Transcribes** every word, adding timestamps like a meticulous librarian.

- **Searches** for keywords faster than you can say "Ctrl+F".

- **Deploys** to the cloud, making it accessible anytime, anywhere.

Step 2: Spring Boot—Not Just for Flowers

We'll use Spring Boot to build a user interface so friendly, even your grandma could use it. Think of it as the welcoming front porch to our transcription mansion.

Step 3: Python—The Snake That Speaks

Behind the scenes, Python will do the heavy lifting:

- **FFmpeg** will extract audio from videos, like squeezing juice from oranges.

- **Speech Recognition** will convert audio to text, turning sounds into words.

- **Timestamps** will be added, marking every significant moment like a historian.

Step 4: Cloud Nine with GCP

Finally, we'll send our creation to the cloud using Google Cloud Platform. It's like giving your app wings to soar and serve users across the globe.

The Encore

By the end of this adventure, you'll have a delightful tool that transforms videos into searchable transcripts, complete with timestamps. It's like having a personal assistant who never sleeps and always knows where that one quote is in that one video.

Ready to roll the cameras and start coding? Let's make some movie magic!

Prerequisites: The Secret Sauce

To cook up this project, you'll need:

1. **Java & Spring Boot**: Think of Spring Boot as the bread holding your application together. It's the framework that lets you build web applications with Java, minus the crusty boilerplate code.

2. **Python & Video Processing Libraries**: Python is the versatile filling—handling tasks like video slicing and dicing using libraries such as OpenCV and FFmpeg.

3. **Google Cloud Platform (GCP)**: This is your delivery service, ensuring your application reaches users far and wide. GCP helps you deploy and scale your app without breaking a sweat.

Learning Resources: Your Culinary School

1. Spring Boot (Java)

- **Official Spring Boot Guide**: A step-by-step tutorial to get your first Spring Boot application up and running.
  (https://docs.spring.io/spring-boot/tutorial/first-application/index.html)

- **GeeksforGeeks Spring Boot Tutorial**: Covers both basic and advanced concepts of the Spring Framework. (https://www.geeksforgeeks.org/spring-boot/)

- **Java Guides Spring Boot Tutorial**: Comprehensive guide covering over 500 topics on Spring Boot. (https://www.javaguides.net/p/spring-boot-tutorial.html)

2. Python Video Processing

- **OpenCV Video Processing Guide**: Learn how to process images of a video using OpenCV.
  (https://www.geeksforgeeks.org/python-process-images-of-a-video-using-opencv/)

- **Cloudinary's Python Video Processing Tutorial**: Explore six useful libraries and a quick tutorial on video processing.
  (https://cloudinary.com/guides/front-end-development/python-video-processing-6-useful-libraries-and-a-quick-tutorial)

- **FFmpeg in Python**: A beginner's guide to using FFmpeg in Python for video processing.
  (https://www.clipcat.com/blog/a-beginners-guide-to-using-ffmpeg-in-python-for-video-processing)

3. Google Cloud Platform (GCP)

- **GCP Quickstarts and Tutorials**: Official tutorials to get started with Google Cloud.

- **FreeCodeCamp's GCP Guide**: A comprehensive guide from zero to hero with GCP.
  (https://www.freecodecamp.org/news/google-cloud-platform-from-zero-to-hero/)

- **GeeksforGeeks GCP Tutorial**: Learn all the basic to advanced concepts of Google Cloud Platform. (https://www.geeksforgeeks.org/google-cloud-platform-tutorial/)

Tools of the Trade

- **Java IDE**: IntelliJ IDEA or Eclipse for Java development.

- **Python IDE**: PyCharm or VS Code for Python scripting.

- **GCP Console**: For deploying and managing your application in the cloud.

Final Thoughts

Embarking on this project is like preparing a gourmet meal. With the right ingredients and recipes, you'll serve up a delectable application that transcribes videos with ease. Bon appétit, coder!

Setting Up Java17 Development Environment

Ahoy, Code Adventurer! Ready to embark on the epic quest of installing Java 17 OpenJDK and Maven across the mystical realms of Windows, Linux, and macOS? Fear not! With this whimsical guide, you'll wield the power of Java and Maven in no time. Let's set sail!

Windows: The Land of Clicks and Wizards

Installing Java 17 OpenJDK

1. **Summon the Installer**: Visit the Microsoft Build of OpenJDK (https://learn.microsoft.com/en-us/java/openjdk/download) and download the Windows MSI for Java 17 (https://learn.microsoft.com/en-us/java/openjdk/download?utm_source=chatgpt.com)

2. **Invoke the Installer**: Double-click the `.msi` file and follow the magical prompts. Accept the terms, choose your path, and complete the ritual.

3. **Set the Enchantments**:

   - **JAVA_HOME**: Navigate to *System Properties > Environment Variables*. Under *System Variables*, click *New* and set:

     - **Variable name**: `JAVA_HOME`

     - **Variable value**: Path to your Java installation (e.g., `C:\Program Files\Microsoft\jdk-17`)

   - **Path**: Edit the `Path` variable and add `%JAVA_HOME%\bin` to the list.

4. **Verify the Spell**: Open Command Prompt and type:
   ```
   java -version
   ```
If the Java version appears, the spell was successful!

Installing Maven

1. **Download the Artifact**: Head to the Apache Maven Downloads
   (https://maven.apache.org/download.cgi) page and fetch the latest binary zip archive.

2. **Unleash the Archive**: Extract the zip to a location of your choice (e.g., `C:\Program Files\Apache\Maven`).

3. **Set the Enchantments**:

   - **MAVEN_HOME**: In *Environment Variables*, create a new system variable:

     - **Variable name**: `MAVEN_HOME`

     - **Variable value**: Path to your Maven directory.

   - **Path**: Edit the `Path` variable and add `%MAVEN_HOME%\bin`.

4. **Verify the Spell**: Open Command Prompt and type:
   ```
   mvn -version
   ```

Behold the Maven version, confirming your success!

Linux: The Realm of Terminals and Penguins

Installing Java 17 OpenJDK

1. **Update the Scrolls**: Open your terminal and run:
   ```
   sudo apt update
   ```
2. **Install Java 17**: Invoke the following command:
   ```
   sudo apt install openjdk-17-jdk
   ```
3. **Set the Enchantments**:
   - **JAVA_HOME**: Add the following to your `~/.bashrc` or `~/.zshrc`:
     ```
     export JAVA_HOME=/usr/lib/jvm/java-17-openjdk-amd64
     export PATH=$JAVA_HOME/bin:$PATH
     ```
   - Apply the changes:
     ```
     source ~/.bashrc
     ```
   -
4. **Verify the Spell**: Type:
   ```
   java -version
   ```
The Java version should reveal itself!

Installing Maven

1. **Install Maven**: Use the package manager:
   ```
   sudo apt install maven
   ```
2. **Verify the Spell**: Type:
   ```
   mvn -version
   ```

Maven's version should appear, signaling success!

MacOS: The Kingdom of Apples and Command Lines

Installing Java 17 OpenJDK

1. **Install Homebrew** (if not already installed): Open Terminal and run:
   ```
   /bin/bash -c "$(curl -fsSL
   https://raw.githubusercontent.com/Homebrew/install/HEAD/install.sh)"
   ```
2. **Install Java 17**: Use Homebrew to install:
   ```
   brew install openjdk@17
   ```
3. **Set the Enchantments**:
   - Add the following to your ~/.zshrc or ~/.bash_profile:
     ```
     export JAVA_HOME=$(/usr/libexec/java_home -v17)
     export PATH=$JAVA_HOME/bin:$PATH
     ```
     - Apply the changes:
       ```
       source ~/.zshrc
       ```
4. **Verify the Spell**: Type:
   ```
   java -version
   ```

The Java version should greet you!

Installing Maven

1. **Install Maven**: Use Homebrew:
   ```
   brew install maven
   ```
2. **Verify the Spell**: Type:
   ```
   mvn -version
   ```

Maven's version should appear, confirming your mastery!

Congratulations, Brave Developer! You've successfully installed Java 17 OpenJDK and Maven across all major realms. May your code compile without errors, and your builds be ever successful!

Setting up Python and Jupyter Lab for Validating Python Code

Let's embark on the whimsical journey of setting up JupyterLab across Windows, Linux, and macOS.

Windows: The Land of Wizards and Installers

Step 1: Install Python

- Download the latest Python installer from the official Python website.

- Run the installer and ensure you check the box that says "Add Python to PATH" before clicking "Install Now."

Step 2: Verify Python and pip Installation

- Open Command Prompt and type:
  ```
  python --version
  pip --version
  ```

- If both commands return version numbers, you're good to go!

Step 3: Install JupyterLab

- In the Command Prompt, type:
  ```
  pip install jupyterlab
  ```
- Wait for the installation to complete.

Step 4: Launch JupyterLab

- Still in the Command Prompt, type:
  ```
  jupyter lab
  ```
- A new browser window should open, displaying the JupyterLab interface.

Linux: The Realm of Terminals and Penguins

Step 1: Install Python and pip

- Open your terminal and type:
  ```
  sudo apt update
  sudo apt install python3 python3-pip
  ```

Step 2: Verify Python and pip Installation

- In the terminal, type:
  ```
  python3 --version
  pip3 --version
  ```

- Ensure both commands return version numbers.

Step 3: Install JupyterLab

- In the terminal, type:
  ```
  pip3 install jupyterlab
  ```

Step 4: Launch JupyterLab

- In the terminal, type:
  ```
  jupyter lab
  ```
- Your default browser should open with the JupyterLab interface.

MacOS: The Kingdom of Apples and Command Lines

Step 1: Install Homebrew (if not already installed)

- Open Terminal and type:
  ```
  /bin/bash -c "$(curl -fsSL
  https://raw.githubusercontent.com/Homebrew/install/HEAD/install.s
  h)"
  ```

Step 2: Install Python

- In Terminal, type:
  ```
  brew install python
  ```

Step 3: Verify Python and pip Installation

- In Terminal, type:
  ```
  python3 --version
  pip3 --version
  ```

- Ensure both commands return version numbers.

Step 4: Install JupyterLab

- In Terminal, type:
  ```
  pip3 install jupyterlab
  ```

Step 5: Launch JupyterLab

- In Terminal, type:
  ```
  jupyter lab
  ```
- Your default browser should open with the JupyterLab interface.

Congratulations, Brave Developer! You've successfully set up JupyterLab on your system. May your data be clean and your plots be pretty!

Setting up yt-dlp for Video Processing

Windows: The Land of Wizards and Installers

Step 1: Summon yt-dlp

- Download the latest `yt-dlp.exe` from the official yt-dlp GitHub releases page (https://github.com/yt-dlp/yt-dlp).

- Place `yt-dlp.exe` in a directory of your choice, such as `C:\yt-dlp`.

Step 2: Optional Magic – Install FFmpeg

- Download the latest FFmpeg build for Windows (https://github.com/yt-dlp/FFmpeg-Builds).

- Extract the files and locate `ffmpeg.exe` and `ffprobe.exe` inside the `bin` folder.

- Copy these two files into the same directory as `yt-dlp.exe`.

Step 3: Add to the PATH of Destiny

- Open the Start Menu and search for "Environment Variables".

- Click on "Edit the system environment variables".

- In the System Properties window, click on "Environment Variables...".

- Under "System variables", find and select the "Path" variable, then click "Edit".

- Click "New" and add the path to your `yt-dlp` directory (e.g., `C:\yt-dlp`).

- Click "OK" to close all windows.

Step 4: Test the Spell

- Open Command Prompt and type:
  `yt-dlp --version`
- If the version number appears, your spell was successful!

Linux: The Realm of Terminals and Penguins

Step 1: Update Your Scrolls

- Open your terminal and run:
  `sudo apt update`

Step 2: Install yt-dlp

- Run the following command:
  `sudo apt install yt-dlp`

Step 3: Optional – Install FFmpeg

- To enable advanced features, install FFmpeg:
  ```
  sudo apt install ffmpeg
  ```

Step 4: Test the Spell

- In the terminal, type:
  ```
  yt-dlp --version
  ```
- If the version number appears, your installation is complete!

MacOS: The Kingdom of Apples and Command Lines

Step 1: Install Homebrew (if not already installed)

- Open Terminal and run:
  ```
  /bin/bash -c "$(curl -fsSL
  https://raw.githubusercontent.com/Homebrew/install/HEAD/install.s
  h)"
  ```

Step 2: Install yt-dlp

- Use Homebrew to install yt-dlp:
  ```
  brew install yt-dlp
  ```

Step 3: Optional – Install FFmpeg

- For enhanced functionality, install FFmpeg:
  ```
  brew install ffmpeg
  ```

Step 4: Test the Spell

- In Terminal, type:
  ```
  yt-dlp --version
  ```
- If the version number appears, your installation is successful!

Congratulations, Brave Developer! You've successfully installed yt-dlp on your system. May your downloads be swift and your videos plentiful!

Setting Up GIT

Windows: The Land of Wizards and Installers

Step 1: Summon the Git Installer

- Download the latest Git for Windows installer from the official Git website (https://git-scm.com/).

Step 2: Run the Installer

- Double-click the downloaded `.exe` file.

- Follow the installation wizard:

    - Choose your preferred editor (e.g., Vim, Notepad++).

    - Select "Git from the command line and also from 3rd-party software".

    - Use the default settings for the remaining options unless you have specific preferences.

Step 3: Verify the Installation

- Open "Git Bash" from the Start menu.

- Type:
  ```
  git --version
  ```
- If Git responds with its version number, the installation was successful!

Step 4: Configure Git

- Set your user name and email:
  ```
  git config --global user.name "Your Name"
  git config --global user.email "you@example.com"
  ```
- Verify your configuration:
  ```
  git config --list
  ```

Step 1: Update Your Package Index

- Open your terminal and run:
  ```
  sudo apt update
  ```

Step 2: Install Git

- Install Git using your package manager:
  ```
  sudo apt install git
  ```

Step 3: Verify the Installation

- Check the installed version:
  ```
  git --version
  ```

Step 4: Configure Git

- Set your user name and email:
  ```
  git config --global user.name "Your Name"
  git config --global user.email "you@example.com"
  ```
- Verify your configuration:
  ```
  git config --list
  ```

MacOS: The Kingdom of Apples and Command Lines

Step 1: Check for Git

- Open the Terminal and type:
  ```
  git --version
  ```
- If Git is not installed, you'll be prompted to install the Xcode Command Line Tools. Follow the on-screen instructions.

Step 2: Alternatively, Install via Homebrew

- If you prefer using Homebrew:

- Install Homebrew if you haven't already:
  ```
  /bin/bash -c "$(curl -fsSL https://raw.githubusercontent.com/Homebrew/install/HEAD/install.sh)"
  ```

- Install Git:
  ```
  brew install git
  ```

Step 3: Verify the Installation

- Check the installed version:
  ```
  git --version
  ```

Step 4: Configure Git

- Set your user name and email:
  ```
  git config --global user.name "Your Name"
  git config --global user.email "you@example.com"
  ```
- Verify your configuration:
  ```
  git config --list
  ```

Congratulations, Brave Developer! You've successfully set up Git on your system. May your commits be frequent and your merge conflicts be few!

Installing MongoDB

Windows: Click, Install, Reboot, Repeat

Step 1: Get the Installer

Go to MongoDB's official download center (https://www.mongodb.com/try/download/community) and download the **MSI installer** for Windows. Make sure to pick the latest Community version.

Step 2: Run the Magical Installer

- Double-click the `.msi` file.

- Choose **"Complete"** installation. Because we're not here for half-baked databases.

- **Tick the box** for "Install MongoDB as a Service." Let Windows handle the startup rituals.

Step 3: (Optional but Powerful) Install MongoDB Compass

This GUI is like a telescope for peeking into your MongoDB collections. Highly recommended for folks who like clicking over typing.

Step 4: Add MongoDB to the PATH

If the installer didn't do it for you, add this to your system environment variables:

```
C:\Program Files\MongoDB\Server\<version>\bin
```

Step 5: Verify It

Open Command Prompt and run:

bash
CopyEdit

```
mongod --version
```

If it talks back, MongoDB is alive!

Linux (Ubuntu/Debian): Where Copy-Paste Is King

Step 1: Import the Public Key

```
wget -qO - https://pgp.mongodb.com/server-6.0.asc | sudo apt-key add -
```

Step 2: Add MongoDB Repo

```
echo "deb [ arch=amd64,arm64 ] https://repo.mongodb.org/apt/ubuntu
$(lsb_release -sc)/mongodb-org/6.0 multiverse" | sudo tee
/etc/apt/sources.list.d/mongodb-org-6.0.list
```

Step 3: Install It

```
sudo apt update
sudo apt install -y mongodb-org
```

Step 4: Start the Sorcery

```
sudo systemctl start mongod
sudo systemctl enable mongod
```

Step 5: Confirm It's Alive

```
mongod --version
```

Bonus:

```
mongo
```

gets you into the Mongo shell (like talking directly to the database. Very Gandalf-y.)

MacOS: For Cool Developers with iTerm2 and Brew

Step 1: Brew It!

```
brew tap mongodb/brew
brew install mongodb-community@6.0
```

Step 2: Start the Daemon

```
brew services start mongodb-community@6.0
```

Or to run manually:

```
mongod --config /usr/local/etc/mongod.conf
```

Step 3: Verify It's Working

```
mongod --version
```

You can also run:

```
mongo
```

And boom! You're inside your new NoSQL playground.

Final Notes (aka Ancient Wisdom)

- The default port is `27017`. Don't fight it unless you really want to.

- MongoDB data files typically live at `/data/db` (or `%ProgramFiles%\MongoDB\Server\...\data` on Windows).

- Keep mongod running like your favorite fantasy server—always in the background, always watching.

CHAPTER 2: Transcribers Assemble: Endgame for Untagged Video Content

Let's delve into the directory structure of the video-transcript-generator (https://github.com/priyeshkpandey/video-transcipt-generator) repository and understand the purpose of each component:

Project Root

- `pom.xml`: This is the Maven Project Object Model file, which manages project dependencies, build configurations, and plugins for the Java-based components of the application.

- `requirements.txt`: Specifies the Python dependencies required for the project. This file allows for easy installation of necessary Python packages using pip.

- `.gitignore`: Lists files and directories that should be ignored by Git. This typically includes build artifacts, temporary files, and other non-essential items that shouldn't be tracked in version control.

- `transcript_generator.py`: A standalone Python script responsible for processing video files and generating transcripts. It likely utilizes libraries such as `yt-dlp` for downloading videos and `whisper` for transcription.

pom.xml

The `pom.xml` file in the `video-transcript-generator` project serves as the backbone of the application's build and dependency management system, leveraging Maven to orchestrate the project's lifecycle. This configuration file outlines the project's metadata, dependencies, build plugins, and other settings essential for compiling, testing, and deploying the application.

Project Metadata

At the outset, the `pom.xml` defines the project's coordinates:

- `<groupId>`: Specifies the group or organization the project belongs to.

- `<artifactId>`: Denotes the project's name.

- `<version>`: Indicates the current version of the project.

These identifiers are crucial for uniquely distinguishing the project within a Maven repository.

Dependencies

The `<dependencies>` section enumerates all external libraries and modules the project relies upon. Key dependencies likely include:

- **Spring Boot Starter Web**: Facilitates the development of web applications, including RESTful services.
- **Spring Boot Starter Data MongoDB**: Provides integration with MongoDB persistence API for database operations.
- **Spring Boot Starter Thymeleaf**: Facilitates the development of web page UI.

Each dependency is defined with its group ID, artifact ID, and version, allowing Maven to fetch and include the appropriate libraries during the build process.

Build Plugins

The `<build>` section configures plugins that customize the build process. Notable plugins may include:

- **Spring Boot Maven Plugin**: Enables packaging the application as an executable JAR or WAR file, simplifying deployment.

- **Maven Compiler Plugin**: Specifies the Java version for source and target compatibility, ensuring consistent compilation across environments.

These plugins are instrumental in automating tasks such as compiling code, running tests, and packaging the application for deployment.

Repositories

If the project utilizes dependencies not available in Maven Central, additional repositories are specified within the `<repositories>` section. This ensures Maven can locate and download all necessary artifacts.

Profiles

The <profiles> section allows for defining different build configurations, catering to various environments such as development, testing, or production. Each profile can modify settings like dependencies, plugins, or properties, enabling flexible and environment-specific builds.

Given the project's focus on video transcription and potential integration with cloud services, the `pom.xml` may include configurations for deploying the application to platforms like Google Cloud Platform (GCP). This could involve plugins or settings that facilitate building Docker images, deploying to App Engine, or interacting with other GCP services.

In summary, the `pom.xml` file orchestrates the project's build lifecycle, manages dependencies, and configures plugins essential for developing, testing, and deploying the `video-transcript-generator` application. Its structured approach ensures consistency, reproducibility, and efficiency throughout the development process.

`src/main`

This directory follows the conventional Maven project structure, separating source code and resources.

- **Java Source Files**: Contains the Java classes and packages that make up the backend of the application, possibly built using the Spring Boot framework. These classes handle web requests, business logic, and interactions with other components.

- **Resources**: Includes configuration files, templates, and static assets required by the Java application. This may encompass application properties, HTML templates for the UI, and other resource files.

Purpose of the Directory Structure

The project's structure is designed to facilitate a clear separation of concerns and support a hybrid technology stack:

- **Backend (Java/Spring Boot)**: Managed under the `src/main` directory, the Java components handle the web server functionalities, API endpoints, and serve the frontend UI.

- **Transcription Logic (Python)**: The `transcript_generator.py` script, along with its dependencies specified in `requirements.txt`, manages the core functionality of downloading videos and generating transcripts.

This modular approach allows developers to work independently on different aspects of the application, promoting maintainability and scalability.

Structure of the Code

Let's delve into the directory structure of the `video-transcript-generator` repository, specifically the `src/main/java/com/video/transcript` path. This structure adheres to standard Java conventions, promoting organized and maintainable code. Here's a breakdown of each subdirectory and its purpose:

controller

Purpose: This package contains the REST controllers that handle incoming HTTP requests. They map client requests to appropriate service methods and return responses.

Typical Contents:

- Classes annotated with `@RestController`.

- Methods annotated with `@GetMapping`, `@PostMapping`, etc., to define endpoints.

Example:

```java
@RestController
@RequestMapping("/api/transcripts")
public class TranscriptController {
    // Endpoint methods
}
```

main

Purpose: This package typically contains the main application class that bootstraps the Spring Boot application.

Typical Contents:

- The `main` method to launch the application.

Example:

```java
@SpringBootApplication
```

```java
public class VideoTranscriptApplication {
    public static void main(String[] args) {
        SpringApplication.run(VideoTranscriptApplication.class, args);
    }
}
```

model

Purpose: Holds the domain models or entities that represent the data structure of the application. These classes are often mapped to database tables.

Typical Contents:

- Classes annotated with `@Entity`.

- Fields annotated with `@Id`, `@Column`, etc., to define table mappings.

Example:

```java
@Entity
public class Transcript {
    @Id
    private Long id;
    private String content;
    // Other fields and methods
}
```

repository

Purpose: Contains interfaces that extend Spring Data JPA repositories, providing CRUD operations for the entities.

Typical Contents:

- Interfaces extending `JpaRepository` or `CrudRepository`.

Example:

```java
public interface TranscriptRepository extends
JpaRepository<Transcript, Long> {
    // Custom query methods if needed
}
```

service

Purpose: Houses the service layer, which contains business logic and acts as an intermediary between controllers and repositories.

Typical Contents:

- Classes annotated with `@Service`.

- Methods implementing business operations.

Example:

```java
@Service
public class TranscriptService {
    // Business logic methods
}
```

```
view
```

Purpose: This package is intended for classes related to the presentation layer, such as templates or view models. In a typical Spring Boot application, this could include Thymeleaf templates or other UI components.

Typical Contents:

- View templates (e.g., `.html` files).

- View model classes.

Example:

```java
public class TranscriptViewModel {
    private String title;
    private String content;
    // Getters and setters
}
```

Overall Purpose of the Structure

The directory structure follows the Model-View-Controller (MVC) architectural pattern, which separates concerns within the application:

- **Model**: Represents the data and business logic (`model`, `repository`, `service`).

- **View**: Handles the presentation layer (`view`).

- **Controller**: Manages incoming requests and directs them to appropriate services (`controller`).

This separation enhances maintainability, scalability, and testability of the application.

View Controller

The `TranscriptGeneratorViewController.java` file in the `video-transcript-generator` repository serves as the bridge between the user interface and the backend services. It's a Spring Boot controller that manages HTTP requests related to video transcription.

Location

`src/main/java/com/video/transcript/view/TranscriptGeneratorViewController.java`

Purpose

This controller handles the routing of web requests to appropriate services. It manages the display of the transcription page and processes user inputs, such as video URLs or file uploads, to generate transcripts.

Key Functionalities

1. **Display Transcription Page**: When a user navigates to the transcription page, this controller serves the appropriate view.

2. **Handle Video Input**: It processes user inputs, whether it's a video URL or an uploaded file, and initiates the transcription process.

3. **Display Results**: After processing, it retrieves the generated transcript and displays it to the user.

Integration with Other Components

- **Services**: It likely calls upon service classes that handle the business logic of downloading videos, extracting audio, and generating transcripts.

- **Models**: Utilizes model classes to structure the data passed between the view and the backend.

- **Views**: Returns view names that correspond to HTML templates, facilitating the display of pages to the user.

Example Workflow

1. **User Action**: A user submits a video URL for transcription.

2. **Controller Processing**: The controller receives this request and calls the appropriate service to handle the transcription.

3. **Service Execution**: The service processes the video and generates a transcript.

4. **Result Display**: The controller then adds the transcript to the model and returns the view to display the results to the user.

This controller is a crucial component in the MVC (Model-View-Controller) architecture of the application, ensuring a seamless flow of data and user interaction.

Controller

The `VideoTranscriptController.java` file in the `video-transcript-generator` repository serves as a REST controller within the Spring Boot application. Its primary role is to handle HTTP requests related to video transcription processes.

Location

`src/main/java/com/video/transcript/controller/VideoTranscriptController.java`

Purpose

This controller manages the backend logic for processing video inputs—either via URLs or uploaded files—and generating corresponding transcripts. It acts as an intermediary between the client requests and the service layer that performs the actual transcription.

Key Functionalities

1. **Handling Video URL Inputs**: Processes HTTP POST requests containing video URLs, initiates the download and transcription process, and returns the generated transcript.

2. **Error Handling**: Manages exceptions that may occur during the transcription process, ensuring that appropriate HTTP responses are returned to the client.

Integration with Other Components

- **Services**: Delegates the core transcription logic to service classes that handle downloading videos, extracting audio, and interfacing with transcription tools or APIs.

- **Models**: Utilizes data models to structure the input and output data, ensuring consistency and ease of data manipulation.

- **Repositories**: May interact with repository classes to store or retrieve transcript data from a database, facilitating persistence and retrieval operations.

Example Workflow

1. **User Action**: A client sends a POST request to the `/transcript/enriched` endpoint with a video URL.

2. **Controller Processing**: The `VideoTranscriptController` receives the request, validates the input, and calls upon the appropriate service method to handle the transcription.

3. **Service Execution**: The service layer processes the video, extracts audio, and generates the transcript using tools like Whisper or other transcription services.

4. **Response Delivery**: Upon successful transcription, the controller returns the transcript data to the client in the HTTP response.

This controller is a crucial component in the application's architecture, facilitating the core functionality of converting video content into searchable text transcripts.

Service

The `VideoTranscriptServiceImpl.java` class in the `video-transcript-generator` repository serves as the concrete implementation of the `VideoTranscriptService` interface. This class encapsulates the core business logic required to process video inputs and generate corresponding transcripts.

Location

`src/main/java/com/video/transcript/service/impl/VideoTranscriptService Impl.java`

Purpose

This class is responsible for orchestrating the sequence of operations that transform a video input into a textual transcript. It acts as an intermediary between the controller layer, which handles HTTP requests, and the underlying utilities or external services that perform the actual transcription.

Key Functionalities

1. **Video Input Handling**: Accepts video inputs, which is in the form of URLs, and prepares them for processing.

2. **Audio Extraction**: Utilizes tools or libraries to extract audio streams from the provided video inputs, preparing them for transcription.

3. **Transcription Invocation**: Calls upon transcription utilities or external APIs (such as Whisper or similar services) to convert the extracted audio into text.

4. **Result Compilation**: Gathers the transcribed text, possibly along with metadata like timestamps, and structures it for return to the controller layer.

5. **Error Handling**: Manages exceptions and errors that may occur during the transcription process, ensuring that informative messages are relayed back to the user.

Integration with Other Components

- **Controllers**: The service is invoked by controller classes (such as `VideoTranscriptController`) to process incoming requests and generate responses.

- **Utilities/External Services**: Relies on transcription utilities or external APIs to perform the actual conversion of audio to text.

- **Models**: Uses data models to structure the input and output data, ensuring consistency and ease of data manipulation.

Example Workflow

1. **User Action**: A user submits a video URL or uploads a video file via the application's interface.

2. **Controller Invocation**: The corresponding controller receives the request and calls the `VideoTranscriptServiceImpl` to process the input.

3. **Service Processing**: The service extracts audio from the video, invokes the transcription utility or API, and compiles the resulting text.

4. **Response Delivery**: The transcribed text is returned to the controller, which then sends it back to the user as part of the HTTP response.

This class is essential for maintaining a clean separation of concerns within the application, allowing for modular development and easier maintenance.

Database

The `TranscriptRepository.java` file in the `video-transcript-generator` repository serves as a data access layer, facilitating interactions between the application and the underlying database for transcript-related operations.

Location

`src/main/java/com/video/transcript/repository/TranscriptRepository.java`

Purpose

This interface extends Spring Data MongoDB's `MongoRepository`, providing CRUD (Create, Read, Update, Delete) operations for the `Transcript` entity. By leveraging Spring Data MongoDB, it eliminates the need for boilerplate code, allowing developers to focus on defining custom query methods when necessary.

Key Functionalities

1. **CRUD Operations**: Inherits methods like `save()`, `findById()`, `findAll()`, `deleteById()`, etc., enabling basic database interactions for `Transcript` entities.

2. **Custom Query Methods**: Developers can define custom query methods following Spring Data MongoDB naming conventions. For instance, a method like `findByVideoId(String videoId)` would automatically generate a query to retrieve transcripts based on the provided video ID.

Integration with Other Components

- **Service Layer**: Service classes, such as `VideoTranscriptServiceImpl`, utilize this repository to perform database operations related to transcripts.

- **Controller Layer**: Controllers invoke service methods that, in turn, interact with the repository to fetch or persist data.

Example Workflow

1. **Transcript Generation**: When a user submits a video for transcription, the application processes the video and generates a transcript.

2. **Data Persistence**: The generated transcript is saved to the database using the `save()` method provided by `TranscriptRepository`.

3. **Data Retrieval**: When a user requests to view a transcript, the application retrieves it from the database using methods like `findById()` or custom query methods defined in the repository.

By adhering to the repository pattern, `TranscriptRepository` promotes a clean separation of concerns, enhancing the maintainability and scalability of the application.

Entities

The `model` package in the `video-transcript-generator` repository defines the application's data structures, serving as the blueprint for how data is represented and managed throughout the system. These classes are integral to the application's functionality, facilitating the storage, retrieval, and manipulation of transcript-related data.

Overview of the `model` Package

Located at: `src/main/java/com/video/transcript/model`

This package contains Java classes that represent the core entities within the application. These entities are typically annotated with JPA (Java Persistence API) annotations, enabling seamless integration with the underlying database. In this implementation as it is connecting with MongoDB, the corresponding mongodb persistence annotations are used.

Key Components

1. **Transcript Entity**:

    o **Purpose**: Represents a transcribed segment of a video, including details such as the content, timestamps, and associated metadata.

- ○ **Fields**:

    - `id`: A unique identifier for the transcript entry.

    - `videoUrl`: Video URL of the video.

  - ○ **Annotations**:

    - `@Document`: Marks the class as a MongoDB document.

    - `@Id`: Denotes the primary key of the entity.

2. **Transcript Request Entity**:

   - ○ **Purpose**: Represents the structure of the request to be sent in the API call
   - ○ **Fields**:
     - `videoUrl`: Video URL of the video.
3. **Transcript Response Entity:**
   - ○ **Purpose**: Represents the structure of the response sent back from the API call
   - ○ **Fields**:
     - `videoUrl`: Video URL of the video.
     - `transcript`: The response transcript generated from the video with timestamps.

Integration with Other Layers

- **Repository Layer**: The entities in the `model` package are managed by repository interfaces (e.g., `TranscriptRepository`) that extend Spring Data JPA repositories. This setup provides CRUD operations and custom query methods for the entities.

- **Service Layer**: Service classes (e.g., `VideoTranscriptServiceImpl`) utilize the repositories to perform business logic operations, such as fetching transcripts for a given video or saving new transcript entries.

- **Controller Layer**: Controllers interact with the service layer to handle HTTP requests and responses, ultimately facilitating the flow of data between the client and the server.

Role in the Application

The `model` package is foundational to the application's architecture, enabling:

- **Data Persistence**: By defining entities that map to database tables, the application can persist and retrieve data efficiently.

- **Data Integrity**: MongoDB annotations and constraints ensure that the data adheres to defined schemas and relationships.

- **Scalability**: A well-structured model layer allows for easy expansion and modification as the application's requirements evolve.

In summary, the `model` package encapsulates the data definitions crucial for the application's operation, serving as the bridge between the database and the business logic.

Machine Learning Code

The `transcript_generator.py` script in the `video-transcript-generator` repository serves as a command-line utility for transcribing video files into text with timestamps. It leverages Python's capabilities to process video inputs, extract audio, and generate corresponding transcripts.

Purpose

This script is designed to automate the process of converting video content into textual transcripts. It acts as a standalone tool that can be invoked from the command line, facilitating batch processing or integration into larger workflows.

Key Functionalities

1. **Argument Parsing**: Utilizes Python's `argparse` module to handle command-line arguments, allowing users to specify input video files and output destinations.

2. **Audio Extraction**: Employs tools like `ffmpeg` to extract audio streams from the provided video inputs, preparing them for transcription.

3. **Transcription**: Integrates with transcription utilities or APIs (such as Whisper or similar services) to convert the extracted audio into text.

4. **Output Generation**: Formats the transcribed text, possibly including timestamps, and writes it to the specified output file or directory.

Integration with Other Components

- **Service Layer**: The script may be invoked by methods from service classes (e.g., `VideoTranscriptServiceImpl`) to handle the core transcription logic.

- **External Tools**: Relies on external utilities like `ffmpeg` for audio extraction and may interface with transcription APIs for generating text.

Example Workflow

1. **User Invocation**: A user runs the script from the command line, providing the path to a video file and specifying an output location.

2. **Processing**: The script extracts audio from the video, invokes the transcription utility or API, and compiles the resulting text.

3. **Output Delivery**: The transcribed text is written to the specified output file, completing the transcription process.

CHAPTER 3: Summon the Server: Deploying the Video-to-Transcript Sorcery on GCP

Deploying an application in **Google Cloud Platform (GCP)** is like giving your app a first-class seat on a high-speed cloud rocket. Here's why developers and companies love GCP (besides the free credits and the occasional cool swag):

Top Benefits of Deploying in GCP

1. Scalability That Would Make a Balloon Jealous

GCP scales your application *automagically*. Whether you're serving 10 users or 10 million, GCP ensures your app doesn't break a sweat (or a socket connection).

2. Access to Google's AI & ML Superpowers

Want to transcribe videos, translate languages, or predict what a cat will do next? GCP integrates directly with tools like:

- Vertex AI

- Cloud Speech-to-Text

- Translation API
  All backed by the same AI tech that powers YouTube and Google Search.

3. Rock-Solid Security (Like Fort Knox with Firewalls)

- Google's global infrastructure includes encryption at rest and in transit.

- Identity and Access Management (IAM) gives you full control over who does what.

- Regular audits and compliance certifications mean you're in good hands (unless you give `chmod 777` everywhere—don't do that).

4. Global Infrastructure

Your app can live in **multiple regions** and **zones**, reducing latency and increasing resilience. It's like teleporting your app closer to your users without breaking the space-time continuum.

5. Pay-as-You-Go (Cloud, Not Couch Surfing)

You only pay for what you use. No surprise bills unless you accidentally leave a monster VM running 24/7. (Pro tip: don't do that.)

6. Integrated DevOps & CI/CD Tools

- Cloud Build

- Cloud Run

- Artifact Registry

- Cloud Monitoring & Logging
  All these tools work seamlessly so you can spend less time debugging pipelines and more time yelling "It works!" at your screen.

7. Container & Serverless Nirvana

- Kubernetes Engine (GKE) for container orchestration.

- Cloud Run and App Engine for going serverless (aka: let Google babysit the infra while you nap).

8. Massive Ecosystem of APIs & Services

From Firestore and Cloud SQL to BigQuery and Pub/Sub, you've got a Lego set of powerful tools to build practically anything.

9. Monitoring, Alerts & Insights That Don't Suck

Stackdriver (now part of Cloud Operations suite) helps you:

- Monitor metrics

- Set up alerts

- Debug production issues
  All without needing to summon ancient terminal incantations.

10. It Plays Well With Others

GCP supports hybrid and multi-cloud deployments (e.g., via Anthos), so you're never locked in. It's like dating the cloud but keeping your options open.

Spinning Up an Instance in GCP

Spinning up instances in Google Cloud Platform (GCP) is like summoning a server from the digital heavens — but even wizardry requires a checklist. Here's what you need to have before you can launch your first VM (Virtual Machine) or other compute resources:

Prerequisites for Spinning Up Instances in GCP

1. A Google Account

- Step 0: You need a Gmail or Google Workspace account.

- If you don't have one… are you from an alternate timeline?

2. GCP Project

- Create a GCP project via the Google Cloud Console.

- It's your sandbox where all resources (VMs, storage, APIs, etc.) live.

- You can name it whatever you want, but "My Cool Project" is taken by everyone.

3. Billing Enabled

- Attach a billing account to your GCP project.

- GCP has a **free tier**, and you get **$300 in credits** for new accounts — like Google's way of saying, "Go build something awesome."

You'll need the following roles or permissions:

- `Compute Admin`

- `Service Account User`

- `Viewer` (optional but helpful)

If you're not the GCP project owner, ping your DevOps overlord for access.

5. Enable the Compute Engine API

- GCP doesn't assume you want everything turned on.

- Go to **APIs & Services > Library** and enable **Compute Engine API**.

6. Firewall Rules (for external access)

- By default, VMs aren't accessible from the outside world.

- You'll need to allow traffic on ports like:

    - `22` for SSH

    - `80` for HTTP

    - `443` for HTTPS

Bonus: don't allow port `666` unless your app is *really* metal

7. Define Instance Configuration

- **Machine Type** (e.g., `e2-medium`, `n1-standard-1`)

- **Region/Zone** (e.g., `us-central1-a`)

- **Boot Disk** (e.g., Debian, Ubuntu, or your custom image)

- **Startup Script** (optional wizardry to bootstrap your app)

8. VPC Network Setup

- GCP creates a default VPC for you, but you can define your own.

- VPC includes subnets, firewalls, and all the virtual plumbing.

9. (Optional but Cool) SSH Key Pair

- GCP can generate one for you, or you can provide your own public key.

- This gives you terminal access to your instance like a digital ninja.

10. Cloud CLI Installed (for terminal warriors)

If you're not into clicking through the console:

- Install `gcloud` CLI.

- Run `gcloud init` to configure it.

- Use `gcloud compute instances create` to summon VMs like a pro.

Create Instance to Deploy the Video to Transcript Generator

Step 1: Login to your GCP console

Step 2: Navigate to Compute Engine section

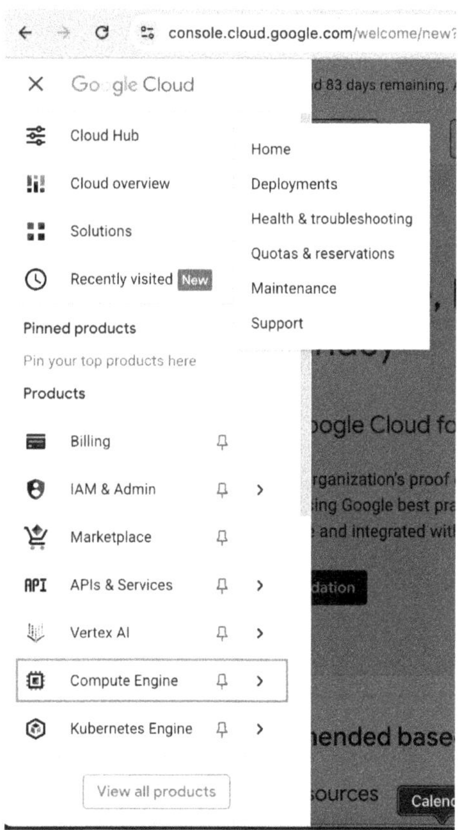

Step 3: Navigate to VM Instances

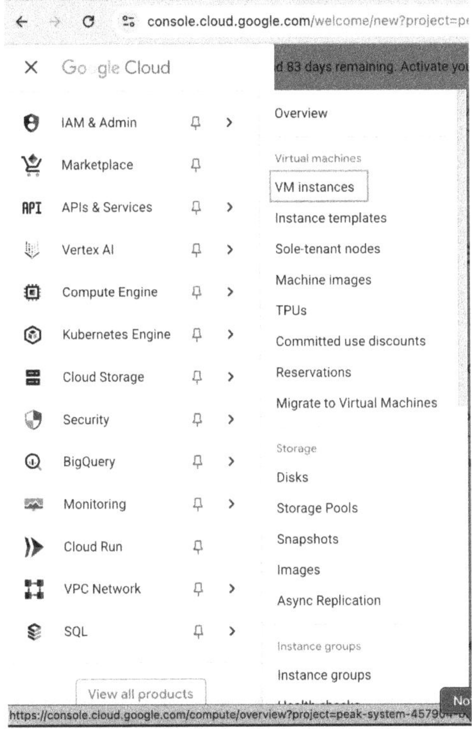

Step 4: Start instance creation by clicking Create instance

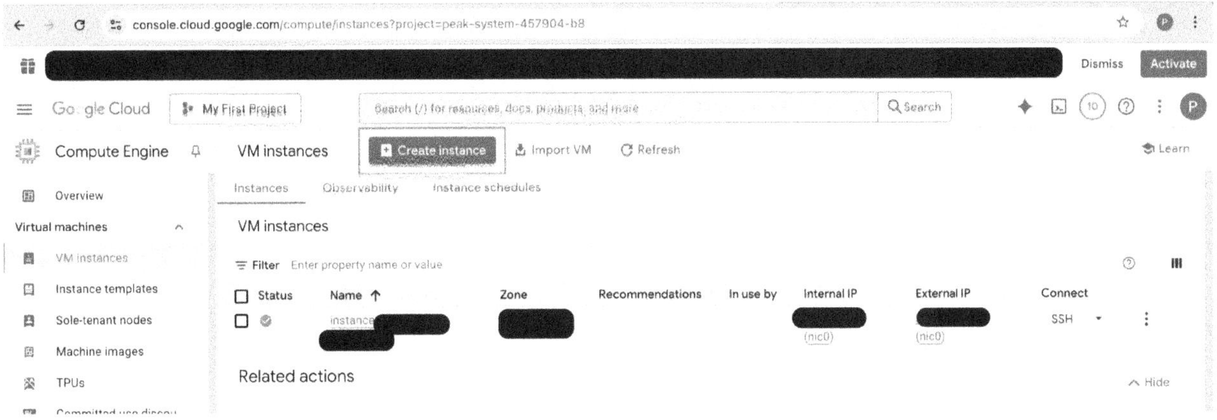

Step 5: It will open the instance creation page

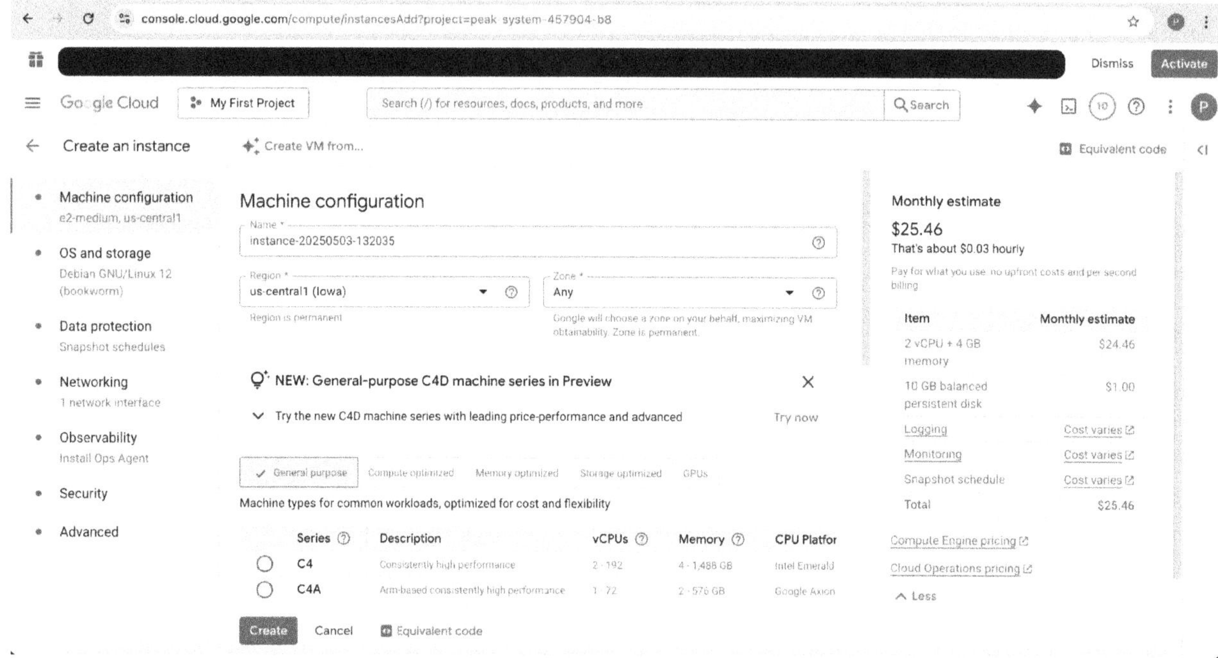

Step 6: Select the instance type as per your need. I have selected a low cost low compute option here.

	Series ⑦	Description	vCPUs ⑦	Memory ⑦	CPU Platfor
○	C4	Consistently high performance	2 - 192	4 - 1,488 GB	Intel Emerald
○	C4A	Arm-based consistently high performance	1 - 72	2 - 576 GB	Google Axion
○	C4D	Preview Consistently high performance	2 - 384	3 - 3,024 GB	AMD Turin
○	N4	Flexible & cost-optimized	2 - 80	4 - 640 GB	Intel Emerald
○	C3	Consistently high performance	4 - 192	8 - 1,536 GB	Intel Sapphire
○	C3D	Consistently high performance	4 - 360	8 - 2,880 GB	AMD Genoa
◉	E2	Low cost, day-to-day computing	0.25 - 32	1 - 128 GB	Intel Broadwe
○	N2	Balanced price & performance	2 - 128	2 - 864 GB	Intel Cascade
○	N2D	Balanced price & performance	2 - 224	2 - 896 GB	AMD Milan
○	T2A	Scale-out workloads	1 - 48	4 - 192 GB	Ampere Altra
○	T2D	Scale-out workloads	1 - 60	4 - 240 GB	AMD Milan
○	N1	Balanced price & performance	0.25 - 96	0.6 - 624 GB	Intel Haswell

Step 7: In the Machine Type section select the size for your CPU.

Machine type

Choose a machine type with preset amounts of vCPUs and memory that suit most workloads. Or, you can create a custom machine for your workload's particular needs. Learn more ⌕

| Preset | Custom |

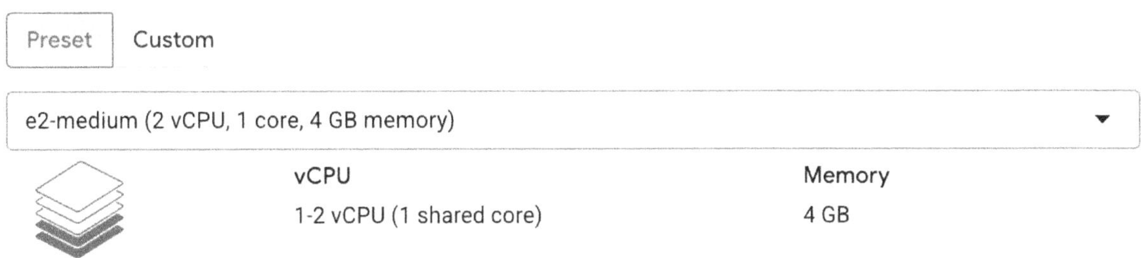

| e2-medium (2 vCPU, 1 core, 4 GB memory) | ▼ |

vCPU
1-2 vCPU (1 shared core)

Memory
4 GB

Step 8: Navigate to the OS and storage and edit as per your storage requirements.

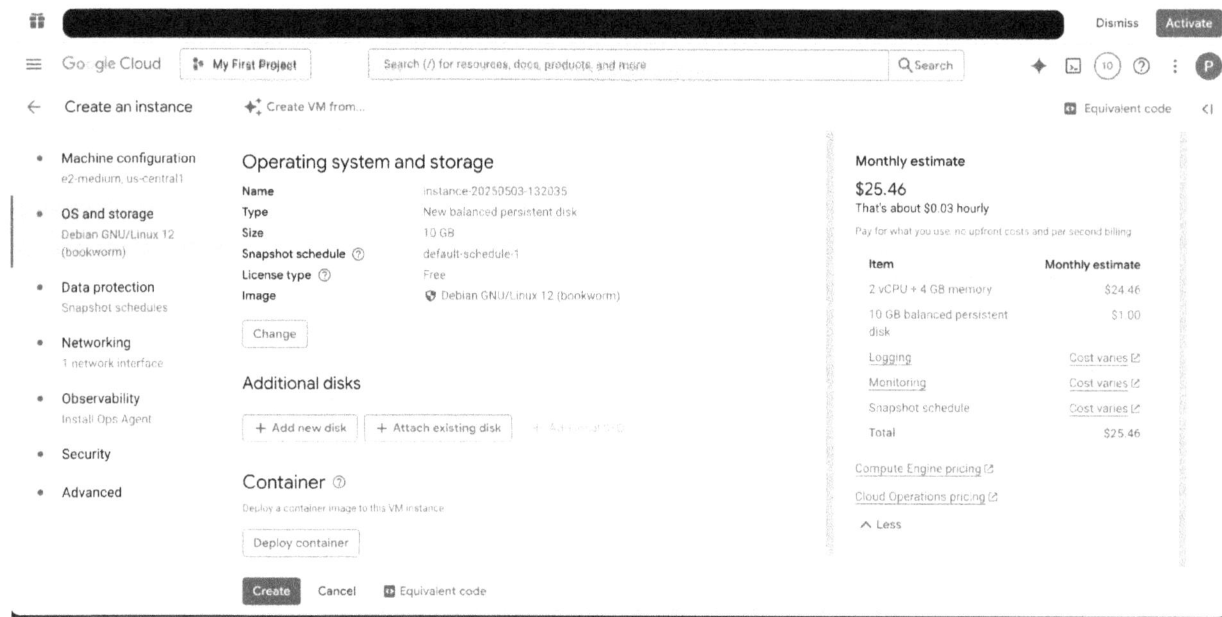

Step 9: Navigate to Networking and allow all types of traffic in the Firewall section.

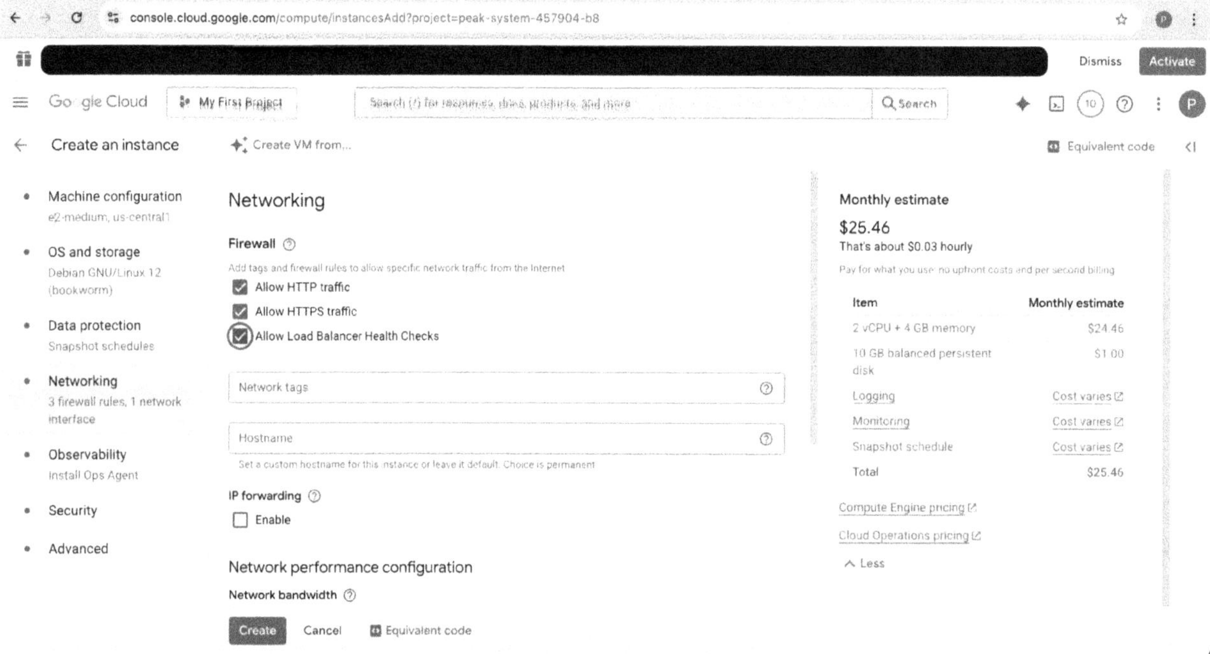

Step 10: Navigate to Network interfaces. In the next few steps I will show how to assign a public IP to your instance. Expand the default network interface.

Network interfaces ⑦

Network interface is permanent

⌄   **default** default IPv4 (10.128.0.0/20)   🗑

Add a network interface

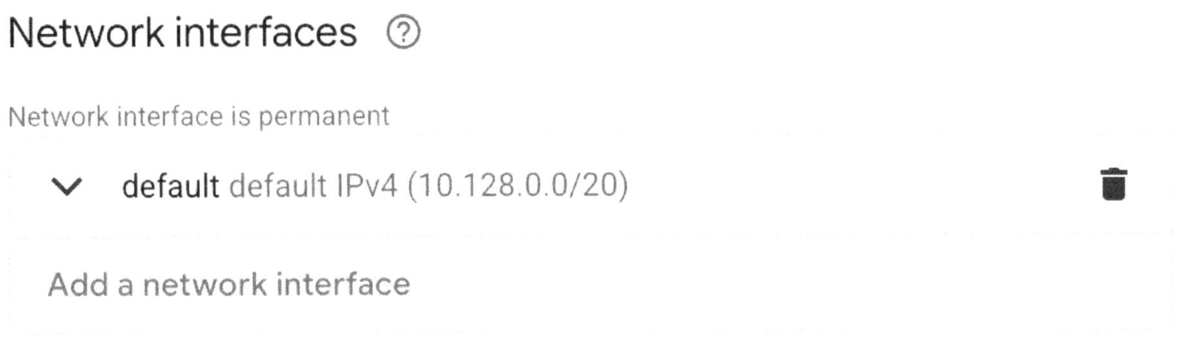

Step 11: Scroll to the External IPv4 address drop down in the default network interface.

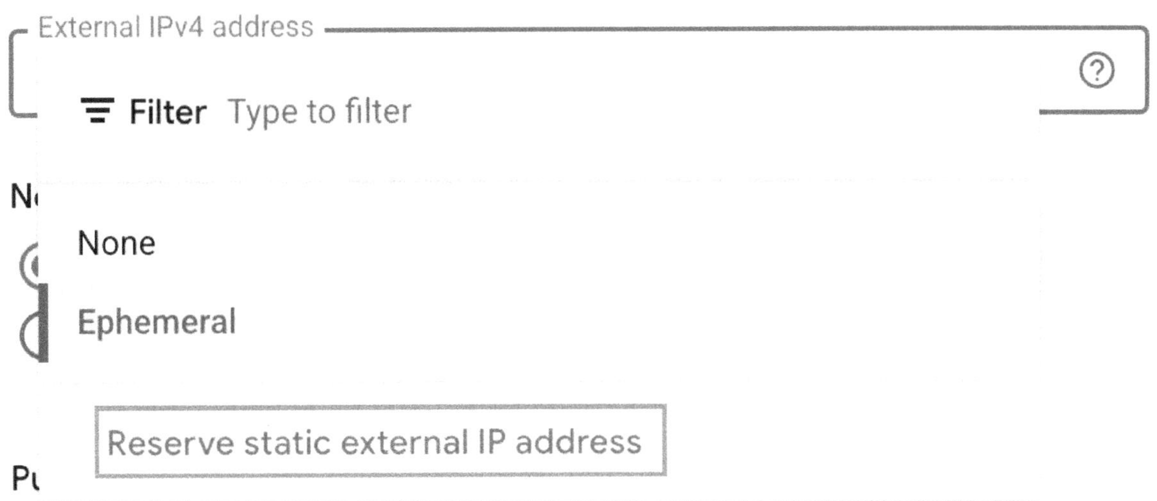

Step 12: Click on the drop down. From the options select Reserve static external IP address

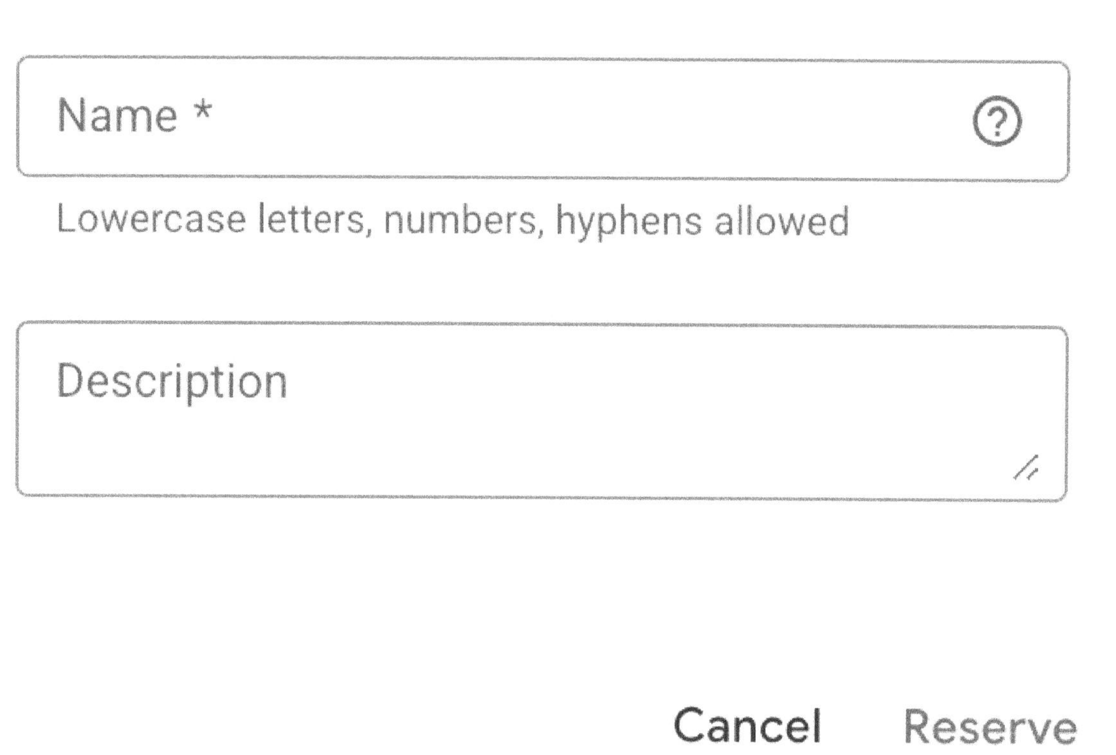
Reserve a static external IP address
Name *
Lowercase letters, numbers, hyphens allowed
Description
Cancel   Reserve

Step 14: Finally launch your instance by clicking the Create button at the bottom of the page.

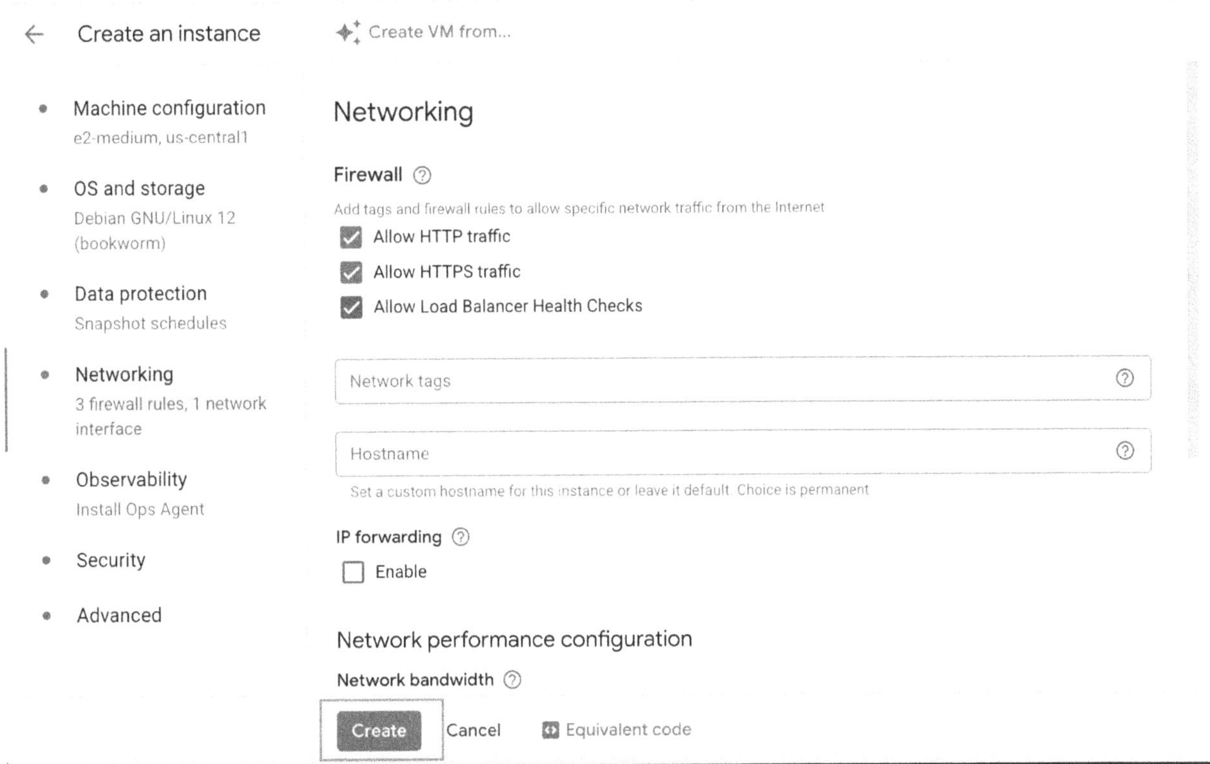

Connecting to Your Instance

Ensure that you have gcloud CLI (Command Line Interface) installed and properly configured by following the instructions at the official GCP documentation page https://cloud.google.com/sdk/docs/install-sdk.

After gcloud is configured, get your gcloud command to SSH into your instance by following below steps.

Step 1: Navigate to VM Instances to see your instance.

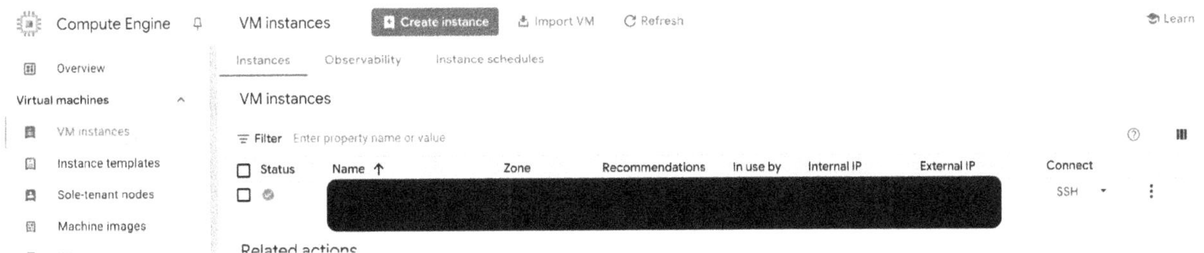

Step 2: Click to expand the SSH options under Connect column. Click View gcloud command from the options.

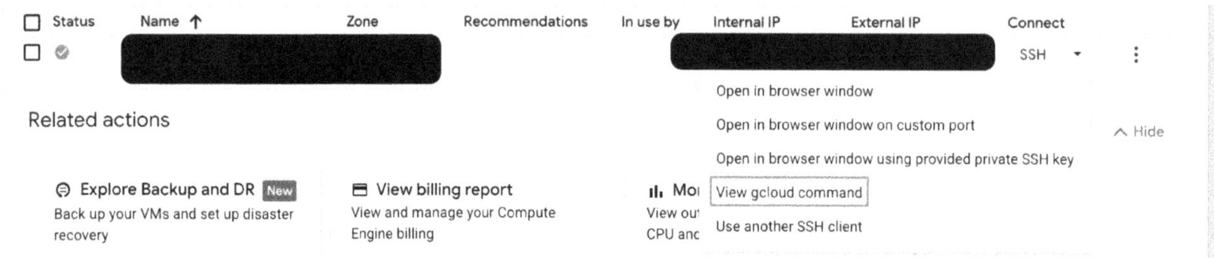

Step 3: Copy the gcloud command shown in the pop up and run on your terminal. You can also select Open in browser window to directly open a SSH session in the browser if you want to skip installation of gcloud CLI.

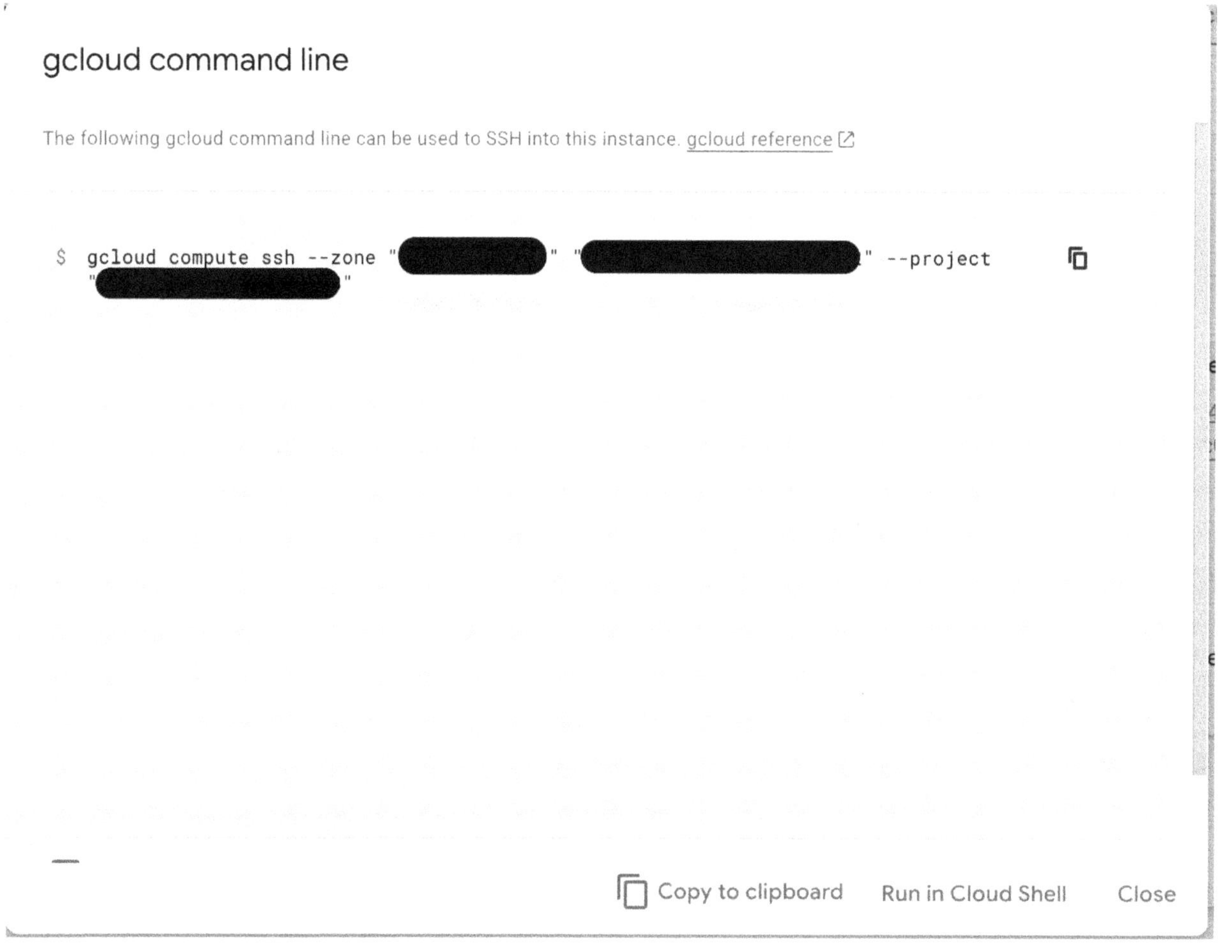

gcloud command line

The following gcloud command line can be used to SSH into this instance. gcloud reference ⊘

```
$  gcloud compute ssh --zone "▉▉▉▉▉" "▉▉▉▉▉▉▉▉▉" --project
   "▉▉▉▉▉▉"
```

Copy to clipboard   Run in Cloud Shell   Close

Deploying the Video-to-Transcript Generator in the GCP Instance

After connecting to your instance do the setups and installations as described in CHAPTER 1.

When done follow the following instructions to clone and deploy the service.

"Clone Wars: GitHub Edition" – Getting the Repo onto Your VM (or local machine)

Step 1: Install Git (if not already installed)

If you try `git` and your terminal says "command not found," it's time to fix that.

Ubuntu/Debian:

```
sudo apt update
sudo apt install git -y
```

macOS (with Homebrew):

```
brew install git
```

Windows (if you're not using WSL or Git Bash):
 Download Git from git-scm.com and install it with wizard-style clicking.

Step 2: Clone the Repository

Now summon the code from GitHub:

```
git clone
https://github.com/priyeshkpandey/video-transcipt-generator.git
```

This command creates a folder named `video-transcipt-generator` and fills it with code like a magic spellbook.

Step 3: Switch to the `gcp-deployment` Branch

Once inside the project directory, switch to the correct branch:

```
cd video-transcipt-generator
git checkout gcp-deployment
```

Boom! You're now riding the GCP-optimized version of the repo

Step 4 (Optional): Verify You're on the Right Branch

```
git branch
```

You should see something like:

```
* gcp-deployment
  main
```

The * means you're on the `gcp-deployment` branch — perfect!

CHAPTER 4: Summary of "Video-Transcript Generator: The Saga of Speech to Searchability"

"From Tutorial to Turmoil: Why Revising Feels Like Time Travel"

- Reliving online courses is hard. Your brain turns into mush, notes look like squirrel scrawls, and memory vanishes faster than free snacks at a tech conference.

- **Solution?** Use AI to generate transcripts with timestamps!

- Like a personal AI secretary (no coffee breaks, no judgment), this tool lets you search keywords in videos and jump straight to "that one part where they explained everything."

"Lights, Camera, Code! Building a Transcript Wizard"

- Walks you through building a full-stack application that:

    - Downloads videos

    - Extracts audio

    - Transcribes to text with timestamps

    - Stores and retrieves via MongoDB

- Java Spring Boot handles the backend, while Python does the AI dirty work using tools like `yt-dlp`, `ffmpeg`, and Whisper.

Architecture Breakdown (MVC Style)

- **Model**: Manages data like transcripts using MongoDB documents.

- **View**: Displays a sleek UI where users can input URLs and see results.

- **Controller**: Handles video uploads and API calls, and delegates tasks to the service layer.

- **Service Layer**: Extracts audio, invokes the AI model, and saves the output.

- **Repository**: Talks to MongoDB like it's fluent in JSON.

Python Scripting with `transcript_generator.py`

- A standalone script that:

    - Parses command-line input

    - Extracts audio using `ffmpeg`

    - Transcribes it using Whisper

    - Outputs beautiful, timestamped text

Perfect for command-line magicians and AI automation nerds alike.

"Summon the Cloud Beast (a.k.a. Deploying to GCP)"

- Deploy the app to Google Cloud Platform to avoid burning out your poor laptop.

- Benefits of GCP:

    - Scalability

    - Pay-as-you-go (until you forget to stop the VM)

    - Serverless options like Cloud Run & App Engine

- Step-by-step guide to spinning up a VM, setting up the environment, and launching your app into the stratosphere of the public cloud.

Bonus Goodies

- **MongoDB Setup** for Windows, Linux, and macOS

- **GitHub Repo Cloning Guide**

- **Funny Dev Commentary** throughout, making it an actual *enjoyable* tech read.

Glossary: Words, Acronyms & Witty Definitions

Video Transcript Generator

A magical tool that converts spoken words in videos into readable, searchable text — because humans weren't meant to click through 3-hour YouTube tutorials to find one definition.

GCP (Google Cloud Platform)

Google's cloud kingdom where you can rent virtual machines, store data, and unleash your app onto the world (or just your boss).

VM (Virtual Machine)

A computer running inside another computer. Like Inception, but for servers.

MongoDB

A NoSQL database that stores data in flexible, JSON-like documents. Basically, it's the cool, laid-back cousin of traditional databases.

Python

A high-level programming language loved for its simplicity, readability, and ability to wrangle AI models without making you cry.

Spring Boot

A Java-based framework that lets you build production-ready web apps with minimal configuration and maximum sass.

ffmpeg

A command-line tool that slices and dices audio/video files like a ninja with a Swiss Army knife.

yt-dlp

A fork of youtube-dl, used to download videos from YouTube and friends. The unofficial "right-click → Save as" of the internet.

Whisper

An AI model by OpenAI that turns speech into text. Basically the AI equivalent of that one classmate who takes excellent notes… in every language.

REST API

A way for apps to talk to each other over the web. It's like a fancy menu that your frontend orders from, and your backend chef prepares.

Thymeleaf

A Java template engine that mixes HTML and Java logic to create dynamic web pages. Think of it as server-side puppetry.

pom.xml

The sacred scroll in every Maven-based Java project. It declares your project's dependencies, plugins, and build rituals.

Maven

A build automation tool for Java. Tells the project what to build, how to test it, and where to keep the chaos (dependencies) organized.

IAM (Identity and Access Management)

Your cloud's bouncer. Grants or denies access to resources based on your role. No badge = no entry.

CLI (Command Line Interface)

The text-only realm where developers feel powerful and non-techies feel nervous.

Git

Version control for your code. Keeps track of all your mistakes — and occasionally your genius.

Transcript

The textual output of the video, often enhanced with timestamps — your shortcut to "that part where the instructor finally explains it properly."